Get to Know

GILA MONSTERS

By Flora Brett

CAPSTONE PRESS
a capstone imprint

First Facts are published by Capstone Press,
1710 Roe Crest Drive, North Mankato, Minnesota 56003
www.capstonepub.com

Library of Congress Cataloging-in-Publication Data
Brett, Flora, author.
Get to know Gila monsters / by Flora Brett.
       pages cm.—(First facts. Get to know reptiles)
Summary: "Discusses Gila monsters, including their physical features, habitat,
range, diet, and life cycle."—Provided by publisher.
Audience: Ages 6–9.
Audience: K to grade 3.
Includes bibliographical references and index.
ISBN 978-1-4914-2061-4 (library binding)
ISBN 978-1-4914-2245-8 (paperback)
ISBN 978-1-4914-2267-0 (ebook PDF)
1. Gila monster—Juvenile literature. I. Title.
QL666.L247B74 2015
597.95'952—dc23
                        2014023858

Editorial Credits
Nikki Bruno Clapper, editor; Cynthia Akiyoshi, designer;
    Svetlana Zhurkin, media researcher; Katy LaVigne, production specialist

Photo Credits
Alamy: Rick & Nora Bowers, 17, 20; Getty Images: Jim Merli, 15 (bottom),
John Cancalosi, 13, Tim Flach, 7; Minden Pictures: NPL/Daniel Heuclin, 19;
Newscom: Imago, 21; Shutterstock: fivespots, cover, 1, 2, 24, Judy Whitton
(background), cover and throughout, Krzysztof Wiktor, 11, reptiles4all, back cover, 5;
SuperStock: All Canada Photos/Jared Hobbs, 9

Printed in the United States   5973

Table of Contents

Monster Myths

Poisonous breath, jaws that never let go, and a deadly bite. Some people have believed these myths about Gila (HEE-lah) monsters. These lizards are named after the Gila River in Arizona. Gila monsters do have venomous, painful bites. But the bites cannot kill people.

Like all lizards, Gila monsters are reptiles. Reptiles have scales and are cold-blooded.

Fact:
Gila monsters' scales cover everything but their bellies. Their scales do not overlap like other lizards' scales do.

venomous—having or producing a poison called venom

reptile—a cold-blooded animal that breathes air and has a backbone; most reptiles have scales

scale—one of many small, hard pieces of skin that cover an animal's body

cold-blooded—having a body temperature that changes with the surrounding temperature

Scales and Tails

Gila monsters' scales look like tiny beads in black, orange, pink, and yellow patterns. Their black eyes blend in with their dark faces. These lizards walk slowly on four short legs. They have rough skin and thick tails. They swing their tails back and forth for balance.

Adult Gila monsters grow to weigh around 5 pounds (2 kilograms). They are 1 to 2 feet (0.3 to 0.6 meter) long.

Fact:

The world's only other venomous lizard is the Mexican beaded lizard. This reptile is a relative of the Gila monster.

Monsters of the Southwest

Gila monsters are found in the southwestern United States. They live in Arizona, California, Nevada, New Mexico, and Utah. They also live in northwest Mexico.

Gila monsters live in desert areas with little water. They make their homes in the Mojave, Sonoran, and Chihuahuan deserts.

Fact:

Gila monsters usually live alone. But they gather in groups in late spring to mate.

North
America

Europe

Asia

Africa

South
America

N
W   E
S

Australia

Where Gila Monsters Live

Antarctica

Gila monster in Arizona

9

Habitats

Gila monsters' habitats are rocky deserts with shrubs. Their burrows are often in rocky foothills. They avoid open areas.

Gila monsters use their strong, curved claws to dig burrows in wet sand. These underground shelters protect Gila monsters from strong heat. Gila monsters leave their burrows at night and hunt for food. They hibernate in their burrows during the winter to stay protected from extreme cold.

Fact:

Gila monsters use their claws to uncover buried food. They can uncover eggs buried 6 inches (15 centimeters) deep.

Gila monster leaving its burrow

habitat—the natural place and conditions in which an animal or plant lives

burrow—a tunnel or hole in the ground made or used by an animal

hibernate—to spend winter in a deep sleep

Monster Meals

Gila monsters use their tongues to smell prey. Their diet includes birds, rodents, bird and reptile eggs, and smaller lizards.

The Gila monster's venom moves through grooves in its teeth. The venom mixes with saliva and the prey's blood. In time, this mix kills or disables the victim. However, Gila monsters often eat their meals very quickly.

Gila monsters may eat only three huge meals all year. They store extra fat in their tails. They use the fat when food is unavailable.

Fact:
Hormones in Gila monsters' venom are used to help people with diabetes.

Gila monster eating a deer mouse

prey—an animal hunted by another animal for food

rodent—a mammal with long front teeth used for gnawing; rats, mice, and squirrels are rodents

Producing Young

Gila monsters mate in late spring. A male raises his body to get a female's attention. Two males may fight to mate with one female. They might wrestle for hours before one male gives up.

After mating the female digs a burrow. She lays 3 to 12 eggs in the burrow and covers them. She then leaves the clutch to incubate in the sun. The babies hatch after 4 to 10 months.

mate—to join with another to produce young

clutch—a group of eggs laid at one time

incubate—to keep eggs warm so they hatch

Fact:
Baby Gila monsters use a special egg tooth to slice through the leathery shells.

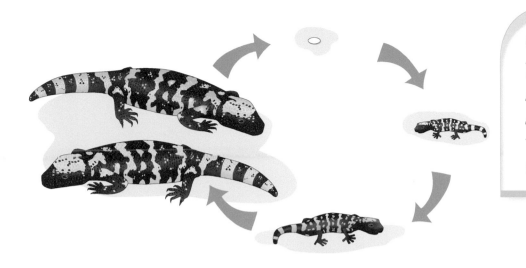

Gila Monster Life Cycle

A Gila monster hatches and becomes an adult. Then it mates and has its own babies.

female Gila monster with her eggs

Growing Up Gila

Hatchlings care for themselves. They search for food at night to stay safe. Predators could easily see the lizards' colorful skin in the daylight.

By age 2 Gila monsters are fully grown. Their yellow skin turns orange and pink as they grow. These darker colors help them blend in with their surroundings. Gila monsters live up to 20 years in the wild and up to 30 years in captivity.

hatchling—a young animal that has just come out of its egg

predator—an animal that hunts other animals for food

captivity—an environment that is not a natural habitat

young Gila monster eating a bird egg

Dangers to Gila Monsters

Hawks, eagles, owls, and other predators swoop down and catch Gila monsters. Coyotes hunt Gila monsters on the ground.

Human actions also threaten Gila monsters. Sometimes people kill Gila monsters because they are afraid of being bitten. Humans move into the areas where Gila monsters live. People also catch Gila monsters and sell them as pets. This illegal practice decreases the number of Gila monsters in the wild. People who sell pet Gila monsters must get permission.

Fact:

Gila monsters use their venom if predators get too close.

Protecting Gila Monsters

Gila monster populations are shrinking. They are considered threatened animals. If their numbers keep shrinking, the reptiles will be at serious risk of dying out. It is not known how many Gila monsters exist today. These shy lizards are rarely seen. It is illegal to kill or to capture Gila monsters in the United States. But we might need to take more steps to protect these amazing lizards.

Amazing but True!

A Gila monster really knows how to use the food it finds. It doesn't eat often, but it can eat one-third of its weight in one meal! Gila monsters also drink a lot at once. They swallow rainwater during summer storms. They store the water in their bladders to use in drier months.

Fact:

Gila monsters move slowly. They sometimes get run over by vehicles on roads.

Glossary

burrow (BUR-oh)—a tunnel or hole in the ground made or used by an animal

captivity (kap-TIH-vuh-tee)—an environment that is not a natural habitat

clutch (KLUHCH)—a group of eggs laid at one time

cold-blooded (KOHLD-BLUHD-id)—having a body temperature that changes with the surrounding temperature

diabetes (dy-uh-BEE-teez)—a disease in which there is too much sugar in the blood

habitat (HAB-uh-tat)—the natural place and conditions in which an animal or plant lives

hatchling (HACH-ling)—a young animal that has just come out of its egg

hibernate (HYE-bur-nate)—to spend winter in a deep sleep

incubate (IN-kyuh-bayt)—to keep eggs warm so they hatch

mate (MAYT)—to join with another to produce young

predator (PRED-uh-tur)—an animal that hunts other animals for food

prey (PRAY)—an animal hunted by another animal for food

reptile (REP-tile)—a cold-blooded animal that breathes air and has a backbone; most reptiles have scales

rodent (ROHD-uhnt)—a mammal with long front teeth used for gnawing; rats, mice, and squirrels are rodents

scale (SKALE)—one of many small, hard pieces of skin that cover an animal's body

venomous (VEN-uhm-us)—having or producing a poison called venom

Read More

Boothroyd, Jennifer. *Endangered and Extinct Reptiles*. Lightning Bolt Books: Animals in Danger. Minneapolis: Lerner Publications Company, 2014.

Clark, Willow. *Gila Monster!* Animal Danger Zone. New York: Windmill Books, 2010.

Ganeri, Anita. *Gila Monster*. Day in the Life: Desert Animals. Chicago: Heinemann Library, 2011.

Internet Sites

FactHound offers a safe, fun way to find Internet sites related to this book. All of the sites on FactHound have been researched by our staff.

Here's all you do:
Visit *www.facthound.com*
Type in this code: 9781491420614

Check out projects, games and lots more at
www.capstonekids.com

Critical Thinking Using the Common Core

1. Gila monsters have unusual eating habits. Explain how these habits help them survive. (Key Ideas and Details)

2. Why do you think people once thought Gila monsters were actual monsters? (Integration of Knowledge and Ideas)

Index